Japanese Reader Collection
LEARN JAPANESE WITH STORIES

Volume 4:
The Mouse Bride
+ Audio Download
and Ikkyū-san

Clay & Yumi Boutwell

Published by Kotoba Books
Copyright © 2010-2021 Kotoba Books

www.TheJapanShop.com
www.TheJapanesePage.com
www.MakotoPlus.com

All rights reserved.

Makoto Monthly E-Zine for Learners of Japanese

誠 MAKOTO
The Fun Japanese Not Found in Textbooks

Japanese lessons and stories with sound files.

It's only a few bucks a month!

https://www.MakotoPlus.com

Download the Latest Makoto Issue | Read 3 Full Back Issues Online | Reusable TheJapanShop.com Coupon | Monthly

INTRODUCTION

The key to learning vocabulary is, quite simply, reading. Not only are you more likely to pick up words that interest you, but you also learn them in context. We hope this book will help with this goal.

FOR UPPER BEGINNERS
These stories are designed for those fairly new to Japanese. The Japanese includes kanji when kanji is commonly used, but we are also including furigana (small kana over kanji) and sound files (see download link in the back) so you can be sure you are reading with the correct pronunciation.

If you are very new to Japanese, please see our Beri- Beri- Shoshinsha digital bundle at thejapanshop.com/bundles

MP3s
Included, at no extra charge, are MP3 sound files of the stories. One is read at the normal speed and the other at a slow, easy to follow speed. If the MP3s were not included when you purchased this book, please see the last page for

a download link. If you have ANY trouble downloading, please email us at help@thejapanshop.com.

ABOUT THIS BOOK

This book contains several versions of each story. First, we have the story with every vocabulary word defined and explained. Next, we go through major grammatical patterns found in the story. After that, read the story with no English and in natural Japanese. Lastly, we are including a simple English translation, which should be avoided until you are sure you understand the story or if you find it too difficult to figure out on your own.

You may want to try to read the story in natural Japanese first. Or if you are a beginner, it may be better to go through the vocabulary first. Any way you do it, this book offers several ways to read, listen, and learn.

Lastly, we would love to hear from you. If you have any suggestions to make this and other books better, please let us know.

Clay & Yumi Boutwell
help@thejapanshop.com
http://www.TheJapanShop.com
http://www.TheJapanesePage.com

P.S. Please see the last page to find the download link for the MP3s of these stories free of charge.

Table of Contents

Makoto Monthly E-Zine for Learners of Japanese ii

INTRODUCTION iii

The Mouse Bride with Definitions vi

Mouse Bride Grammatical Notes 23

The Mouse Bride *in Japanese* 30

The Mouse Bride *English Summary* 35

Ikkyū-san with Definitions 37

Ikkyu-san Grammatical Notes 50

Ikkyū-san in Japanese 56

Ikkyū-san in English 60

VOCABULARY 62

DOWNLOAD LINK 71

The Mouse Bride with Definitions

ねずみの嫁入り
<ruby>嫁<rt>よめ</rt></ruby>

Story Read Slowly

Story Read Normal Speed

Scan the QR codes for instant and FREE access to audio recordings

むかし、むかし、あるところに
ねずみのお父さん、お母さんが住んでいました。二人は、一人娘の
チュー子をたいへんかわいがっていました。

むかしむかし a long time ago
あるところに some place
ねずみ mouse
お父さん father
ねずみのお父さん the father mouse
お母さん mother
住んでいました there lived...
二人 the two (mice)
一人 one person
娘 daughter
一人娘 one and only daughter
娘のチュー子 a daughter named Chu-ko
たいへん very
かわいがっていました loved; tender loving care [from かわいがる]

この 娘
むすめ
は、とても美人でお父さんと
びじん
とう
お母さんは、いつも自慢ばかりしてい
かあ
じまん
ました。

チュー子が年頃になったので、どこ
こ
としごろ
かお嫁にやることにしました。
よめ

この this
娘 daughter
とても very
美人 beautiful woman
と and
いつも always
自慢 pride; boast(ing)
いつも自慢ばかり always bragging (about daughter)
年頃 of (marriageable) age
になった became [〜になる ˜ni naru to become]
ので therefore
どこか somewhere
お嫁 bride
お嫁にやる give one's daughter in marriage
ことにしました was decided

お父さんは、ある日お母さんと相談しました。

「チュー子は、とても美人だし、きだてのいい子だ。世界で一番偉い人と結婚させよう。」

お父さん father
ある日 one day
お母さん mother
相談 consult; talk it over
とても美人 a very beautiful woman
きだてのいい good natured; kindhearted
子 child
世界で in the world
一番 #1; the best; -est
偉い great; famous
一番偉い人 greatest person (in the world)
と with
結婚 marriage
結婚させよう let's marry her off

おかあさんは、賛成して言いました。

「もちろんですとも。世界で一番偉い人と結婚してほしいですわ。でも、世界で一番えらい人って誰でしょう？」

お母さん mother
賛成 agreement; approval
賛成して言いました agreeing, she said...
もちろん of course
〜とも certainly; of course
もちろんですとも of course! To be sure!
世界で一番偉い人 the world's greatest man
ほしい want; desire
と結婚してほしい want (daughter) to get married to (greatest man)
わ [sentence ender used by women]
でも but
世界で一番えらい人 the world's greatest man
って [casual topic marker: speaking of..., who is he?]
誰 who
誰でしょう who could it be?

おとうさんは、少し考えてから言いました。

「それは、やはり太陽さんだろう。」

お父さん father
少し a little
考えて thinking [考える *kangaeru* to think]
少し考えてから after thinking a little...
言いました said
それは as for that
やはり not surprisingly; as expected; of course, it is...
太陽さん the sun [Mr. Sun]
だろう I suppose

二人は、太陽のところへ出かけていきました。太陽に会うと、ねずみの夫婦は、言いました。

二人 the couple
太陽のところ the sun's place; Where the sun is
へ the direction of
出かけていきました left; went
太陽に会うと upon meeting the sun...
夫婦 husband and wife
言いました said

「世界で一番えらい太陽さん。どうぞ娘をお嫁にもらってください。」

太陽は、びっくりして言いました。

「私が世界で一番えらいだって？

世界で一番えらい太陽さん Sun, who is the greatest in the world...
どうぞ please (take our daughter)
お嫁 bride
お嫁にもらってください please take (daughter) as a bride
太陽 the sun
びっくり surprised
言いました said
私 I
世界で in the world
一番 the best; the most
えらい important
って *[casual topic marker: speaking of...,]*

とんでもない。私は、雲さんにはかなわない。雲さんがでてくれば、私はすっかり隠れてしまうからね。」

そこで、ねずみの夫婦は、雲さんのところへ出かけていきました。

とんでもない absurd; preposterous
私は as for me...
雲さん clouds [Mr. Cloud]
かなわない cannot match; be no match for
雲さんにはかなわない I'm no match for the clouds.
でてくれば if comes out
すっかり completely
隠れてしまう completely hidden
から because [after explanation]
ね [sentence ender to emphasize or show understanding]
そこで then
夫婦 husband and wife
雲さんのところ the Cloud's place; Where the cloud is
へ to
出かけていきました left; went

「世界で一番えらい雲さん、どうぞ娘をお嫁にもらってください。」

雲は、びっくりして言いました。

世界で in the world
一番 the best; the most
えらい important
雲さん clouds [Mr. Cloud]
どうぞ please
娘をお嫁にもらってください please take (our) daughter as a bride
雲 cloud
びっくり surprised
びっくりして言いました surprised, he said...

「私が世界で一番えらいって？とんでもない。私は、風にはかなわない。風が吹けば私は吹き飛ばされてしまうからね。」

私 I
世界で in the world
一番 the best; the most
えらい important
って [casual topic marker]
とんでもない absurd; preposterous
私は as for me, I...
風 wind
かなわない cannot match; be no match for
風 wind
が [particle that often marks the subject]
吹けば if blows [風が吹く wind blows]
吹き飛ばされてしまう blow completely away
から because [after explanation]
ね [sentence ender used for emphasis]

そこで、ねずみの夫婦は、風さんのところへ出かけていきました。

「世界で一番えらい風さん。どうか娘を嫁にもらってください。」

風は、びっくりして言いました。

そこで then
ねずみ mice
夫婦 husband and wife
雲のところ the Cloud's place; Where the cloud is
へ to
出かけていきました left; went
世界で in the world
一番 the best; the most
えらい important
風さん Mr. wind
どうか please [a little more pleading than どうぞ]
娘 daughter
を [direct object marker]
嫁 bride
娘をお嫁にもらってください please take (our) daughter as a bride
風 wind
びっくりして言いました surprised, he said…

「私が世界で一番えらいだって？とんでもない。私は、壁さんにはかなわない。私がいくら吹いても壁さんはびくともしないからね。」

私 I
世界で in the world
一番 the best; the most
えらい important
って [casual topic marker]
とんでもない absurd; preposterous
私は as for me; I...
壁さん wall [Mr. Wall]
にはかなわない no match against...
わたし I; me
が [particle that often marks the subject]
いくら吹いても however much (I) blow
壁さん wall [Mr. Wall]
びくともしない does not budge an inch; unmovable
から because [used to explain something]
ね isn't it [sentence ender to emphasize and prompt for acknowledgement]

そこで、ねずみの夫婦は、壁さんのところへ行きました。

「世界で一番えらい壁さん。どうか娘を嫁にもらってください。」

壁は、びっくりして言いました。

そこで then
ねずみ mouse
夫婦 husband and wife
壁さんのところ where the wall is
〜へ行きました went to ...
世界で in the world
一番 the best; the most
えらい important
壁さん Mr. Wall
どうか please [a little more pleading than どうぞ]
娘 daughter
を [direct object marker]
嫁 bride
娘をお嫁にもらってください please take (our) daughter as a bride
壁 wall
びっくり surprised
びっくりして言いました surprised, he said...

「私が世界で一番えらいだって？とんでもない。私はねずみさんにはかなわない。ねずみは私に穴を開けてしまうからね。」

私 I
世界で *in the world*
一番 the best; the most
えらい important
って [casual topic marker]
とんでもない absurd; preposterous
私は I; as for me...
ねずみ mouse
私はねずみさんにはかなわない I'm no match for the Mouse
ねずみ mouse
私に in me
穴 hole
開ける to open
私に穴を開けてしまう *(mouse) opens holes in me*

ねずみの夫婦は、顔を見合わせてこう言いました。

「なーんだ。ねずみが世界で一番えらいのか。」

ねずみ mouse
夫婦 husband and wife
顔 face
見合わせて look at each other
こう like this
こう言いました said the following
なーんだ What?!
世界で in the world
一番 the best; the most
えらい important
のか [ender showing a realization of the truth)]

そして、ねずみのチュー子さんは、隣村のチュー吉さんと結婚することになりました。

おしまい。

そして and then
ねずみのチュー子さん the mouse Chuko
隣村 the next village
チュー吉 Chukichi
と結婚する get married to...
ことになりました the matter (marriage) happened
おしまい the end

Mouse Bride Grammatical Notes

むかし、むかしあるところに
A long time ago, in a certain place.
This is a very typical opening for Japanese fairy tales similar to "Once upon a time..."

むかし *mukashi*
long time ago [The repetition makes this a very long time ago.]

あるところに *aru tokoro ni*
in a certain place [The ある makes the place undefined like the "some" in somewhere.]

ねずみのお父さん、お母さんが住んでいました
There lived a papa and mama mouse.

ねずみのお父さん *nezumi no otōsan*
papa mouse [This is a common construction for describing someone: The father who is a mouse. くまのプーさん *kuma no pu-san* Winnie the Pooh; となりの山田 *tonari no yamada* Our neighbors, the Yamadas; 赤毛のアン *akage no an* Anne of Green Gables (literally, red-headed Anne)]

住んでいました *sunde imashita*
there lived [This is also often found in the first sentence of a Japanese fairy tale: There lived... Note, the "*i*" in *imashita* is short unlike the longer "*ī*" in *īmashita (said)*.]

二人は、一人娘のチュー子
The two had a single daughter named Chu-ko.

二人は、一人娘 *futari wa, hitori musume*
Counter for people: 一人 *hitori* One person, 二人 *futari* Two people—three people on uses *nin*: 三人 *san nin*, 四人 *yo nin* (notice *yo* not *yon*), 五人 *go nin*…
一人娘 *hitori musume*—One (and Only) daughter

チュー子 *chūko*
子 *ko* is a common ending in female names.

たいへんかわいがっていました
(They) loved (her) very much.

たいへん *taihen*
usually means "very" as in this case. When used alone as in 「たいへんだ。」 it means "trouble" or "I'm doing something difficult."

かわいがっていました *kawaigatte imashita*
loved; showed affection [The parents lavished great love on their only daughter.]

いつも自慢ばかりしていました
They always bragged (about her).

〜ばかり *~bakari* only; nothing but…
Together with いつも, the ばかり reinforces the idea that the parents were constantly bragging about their daughter.

チュー子が年頃になったので
Chu-ko became of age.

年頃になった *toshigoro ni natta*
become of (marriageable) age

ので *node*
that being the case; because of that; therefore [Use ので when giving a reason for an effect. Because of A, B.]

どこかお嫁にやることにしました
(They) decided to give her as a bride to somewhere

お嫁にやる *o yome ni yaru*
give the bride [Just like in English, a bride can be "given."]

ことにする *koto ni suru*
It was decided to do... [The にする is often used when making decisions. ピザにする I'll have (decide upon) pizza.]

お父さんは、お母さんと相談しました
The father and mother talked about it.

と *to*
The と shows who the father consulted (相談) with (お母さん)

チュー子は、とても美人だし
Chu-ko is a real beauty and...

だし... *da shi...*
Used when giving a list of reasons (she's beautiful and well-mannered).

世界で一番えらい人と結婚させよう
Let's marry her to the world's most important person.

一番 *ichiban*
#1; the best; -est: The great**est** man

結婚させよう
させよう ＝ させる (make, have done, let...) ＋ よう
(Imperative): Let's cause her to get married.

もちろんですとも。
Well, of course!

とも *tomo*
A sentence ender stressing agreement.

結婚してほしいですわ
I want her to marry (the world's greatest).

〜してほしい *~shite hoshi*
Want to...

わ *wa*
A feminine ending

世界で一番偉い人って誰でしょう？
Who is the world's greatest person?

って *tte*

Acts as a casual topic marker (similar to は).

やはり太陽さんだろう。
Of course, it must be the sun.

やはり *yahari*

Must be…; As expected… [The father mouse thinks it is understood the Sun must be the greatest, but uses だろう *darou* to show he isn't 100% sure.]

私が世界で一番えらいだって？
I am the world's greatest person?!

って *tte*

As stated above, it acts as a casual topic marker, but it also shows disbelief as a question marker: You think I'm the greatest?!

雲さんにはかなわない
(I'm) no match for Mr. Cloud.

かなわない *kanawanai*

No match

には *niwa*

[The には shows who (the Cloud) the speaker (the Sun) is no match for]

雲さんがでてくれば、私はすっかり隠れてしまうからね。
When Mr. Cloud comes out, I am completely hidden.

出てくれば *dete kureba*
出てくる changes to 出てくれば **If** comes out

しまう *shimau*
(after the て form) shows completion and often regret.

から *kara*
Because [When から appears at the end of a sentence or phrase, it is probably "because" and not the preposition "from."]

私は吹き飛ばされてしまうからね。
I am blown away.

飛ばされる *tobasareru*
To be caused to fly (away)

しまう *shimau*
(after the て form) shows completion and often regret.

いくら吹いても
However much (I) blow.

いくら・・・ても *ikura... temo*
No matter how… (much I blow)

なーんだ。ねずみが世界で一番えらいのか。
What's all this? The mouse is the greatest in the world?!

なーんだ *nanda*

The 一 emphasizes their surprise

一番えらいのか *ichiban erai noka*

の is an abbreviation of のです・のだ and is used to indicate an explanation or show emphasis.

The か makes the sentence into something of a rhetorical question.

The Mouse Bride *in Japanese*

ねずみの嫁入り

むかし、むかし、あるところにねずみのお父さん、お母さんが住んでいました。二人は、一人娘のチュー子をたいへんかわいがっていました。この娘は、とても美人でお父さんとお母さんは、いつも自慢ばかりしていました。

チュー子が年頃になったので、どこかお嫁にやることにしました。

お父さんは、ある日お母さんと相談しました。

「チュー子は、とても美人だし、

きだてのいい子だ。世界で一番えらい人と結婚させよう。」

おかあさんは、賛成して言いました。

「もちろんですとも。世界で一番えらい人と結婚してほしいですわ。でも、世界で一番えらい人って誰でしょう？」

おとうさんは、少し考えてから言いました。

「それは、やはり太陽さんだろう。」

二人は、太陽のところへ出かけていきました。太陽に会うと、ねずみの夫婦は、言いました。

「世界で一番えらい太陽さん。どうぞ

娘をお嫁にもらってください。」

太陽は、びっくりして言いました。

「私が世界で一番えらいだって？とんでもない。私は、雲さんにはかなわない。雲さんがでてくれば、私はすっかり隠れてしまうからね。」

そこで、ねずみの夫婦は、雲さんのところへ出かけていきました。

「世界で一番えらい雲さん、どうぞ娘をお嫁にもらってください。」

雲は、びっくりして言いました。「私が世界で一番えらいって？とんでもない。私は、風にはかなわない。風が吹けば私は吹

き飛ばされてしまうからね。」

　そこで、ねずみの夫婦は、風さんのところへ出かけていきました。
「世界で一番えらい風さん。どうか娘を嫁にもらってください。」

　風は、びっくりして言いました。
「私が世界で一番えらいだって？とんでもない。私は、壁さんにはかなわない。私がいくら吹いても壁さんはびくともしないからね。」そこで、ねずみの夫婦は、壁さんのところへ行きました。

「世界で一番えらい壁さん。どうか娘を嫁にもらってください。」

壁は、びっくりして言いました。

「私が世界で一番えらいだって？とんでもない。私はねずみさんにはかなわない。ねずみは私に穴を開けてしまうからね。」

ねずみの夫婦は、顔を見合わせてこう言いました。

「なーんだ。ねずみが世界で一番えらいのか。」

そして、ねずみのチュー子さんは、隣村のチュー吉さんと結婚することになりました。

おしまい。

The Mouse Bride *English Summary*

Please try to tackle the Japanese first and use this only as needed.

Once upon a time, there was a mouse father and mother. They had a single daughter, Chuuko that they doted on constantly. This daughter was very beautiful and was always a source of pride for her parents. Chuuko had become of age, and they decided to find someone for her to marry.

One day, the father mouse spoke to the mother mouse.

"Chuuko is very beautiful and well mannered. Let's find the world's greatest person for her to marry!"

The mother mouse wholeheartedly agreed.

"Of course! I want her to marry the most important person. But... I wonder who the greatest person in the world is."

The father thought for a moment and then said, "Well, of course, that has to be Mr. Sun."

The two mice left, heading toward the sun.

Upon meeting the sun, the mouse couple said, "Oh, Mr. Sun, thou greatest in the world, please take our daughter to wife!"

The sun, quite surprised, said, "I am the greatest in the world?! Unthinkable! I'm no match for Mr. Cloud. If Mr. Cloud comes out, I am completely hidden."

Then, the mouse couple headed for the cloud.

"Oh, Mr. Cloud, thou greatest in the world, please take our daughter to wife!"

The cloud, surprised, said, "I am the greatest in the world?! Unthinkable! I cannot stand against Mr. Wind. As the wind blows, I get blown away."

Then, the mouse couple headed toward the wind.

"Oh, Mr. Wind, thou greatest in the world, please take our daughter to wife!"

The wind, surprised, said, "I am the greatest in the world?! Outrageous! I cannot stand up to Mr. Wall. No matter how much I blow, Mr. Wall doesn't move."

Then, the mouse couple headed toward the wall.

"Oh, Mr. Wall, thou greatest in the world, please take our daughter to wife!"

Mr. Wall, surprised, said, "Me, the greatest in the world?! Not in the least! I am no match for the mouse. Mice open holes in me."

The mouse couple looked at each other and said, "What? A mouse is the greatest in the world?"

Then, the mouse Chuuko married a mouse named Chuukichi from a neighboring village.

The End.

Ikkyū-san with Definitions

いっきゅう
一休さん

Story Read Slowly

Story Read Normal Speed

Scan the QR codes for instant and FREE access to audio recordings

むかし、むかし、一休(いっきゅう)さんというとても賢(かしこ)いお坊(ぼう)さんがいました。小(ちい)さいころから、賢(かしこ)くてりこうだと評判(ひょうばん)でした。

むかし、むかし a long time ago
一休さん [a name]
という "such a"; (describing ikkyuu-san)
とても very
賢い wise
お坊さん priest; monk; young boy
〜がいました there lived; there was...
小さいころ when one was a child; childhood
から from (childhood)
賢くてりこう wise and clever [*kashikoi* is paired with the similar-in-meaning 利口 *rikō*—wise; clever; intelligent]
評判 fame; reputation

これは、一休(いっきゅう)さんが子供(こども)のころのお話(はなし)です。

これは as for this (story)
一休さん Ikkyu
子供のころ childhood
お話 story (polite)

一休さんの賢さの評判を聞いた将軍様は、一休さんを困らせてやろうと思って、ある日、一休さんをお城に呼んで、こう言いました。

賢さ level of wisdom [〜さ indicates a degree or condition of something]
賢さの評判 reputation for having wisdom
聞いた heard [past tense of 聞く *kiku*—to listen]
将軍様 a general; military leader (honorific)
困らせてやろう to try to trouble (Ikkyu) [*komarasete*—to trouble with questions; to test + *yarō*—to do; to give (trouble)]
と思って (he) thought
ある日 one day
お城に castle (honorific)
呼んで called (to the castle)
こう言いました said the following

「一休さん、そちに頼みたいことがあるのだが。」そういって、一枚のびょうぶを見せました。そのびょうぶには、一匹の虎が描かれていました。

そちに for you [*sochi* means there or that way, but in this case, the shogun is referring to Ikkyu.]
頼みたいこと a request; something to ask
がある (I) have (a request)
だが but [a polite way to soften a request.]
そういって saying that...
一枚 one (byobu)
びょうぶ *a* folding screen; byobu
見せました showed
その that (byobu)
一匹 one (tiger) [hiki/biki/piki is the counter for animals]
虎 tiger
描かれていました was drawn

「この虎が、毎晩抜け出して、いたずらをするので、困っている。なんとか、この虎を捕まえたいのだ。」

この this
虎 tiger
が particle usually indicating the subject
毎晩 every night
抜け出して sneak out; slip away
いたずら prank; mischief; tricking
ので because (the tiger did pranks)
困っている was troubled
なんとか somehow; one way or another
捕まえたい want to capture
のだ (explanatory ender + copula)

絵に描いた虎を捕まえることなんて、できるわけがありません。一休さんは、しばらく考えてからこう言いました。

絵に in the picture
描いた drawn
捕まえること (the act of) capturing
なんて (exclamation; emphatic) how ...!
できる being able to do
わけがありません have to reason (to be able to)
一休さん Ikkyu
しばらく a while; some time
考えて thinking
しばらく考えてから after thinking a while
こう言いました said thusly

「かしこまりました。」一休(いっきゅう)さんは、立ち上(た-あ)がって頭(あたま)にねじりはちまきをしめ、なわをもってびょうぶの前(まえ)に立(た)ちました。

かしこまりました understood; roger that
立ち上がって standing up... [this is combining *tachi* (stand) with *agaru* (raising) in the ~*te* form]
頭 head
ねじり twist
はちまき headband
しめ tighten; bind
頭にねじりはちまきをしめ tightening the headband around his head
なわ rope; cord
もって holding (the rope)
びょうぶ folding screen
前に in front of
立ちました stood

将軍様、私は用意ができました。いつでも虎を捕まえましょう。さあ、将軍様、そのびょうぶの虎をそこから追い出してください。」

将軍様 General [*sama* is polite]
私は as for me, I...
用意 preparations
用意ができました I'm ready; I'm prepared
いつでも whenever
虎 tiger
を [direct object marker]
捕まえましょう let's capture (the tiger)
さあ well, then; all right...
そのびょうぶの虎 the tiger in that folding screen
そこから from there
追い出してください please chase (it) out

将軍様は、びっくりして、「なんじゃと、絵に描いた虎を追い出せというのか？」

びっくりして being surprised...
なんじゃと what's that? [*nanja* is colloquial *for nan desu ka* (what's that?) and the *to* is a particle used for quoting and here, to indicate a question.]
絵に in the picture
描いた虎 the painted tiger
追い出せ drive out (imperative)
というのか are you saying...? [*to iu*—saying or such a thing and the emphatic ender *noka*.]

「はい、将軍様。お願いいたします。」将軍様が青くなっていると、一休さんは、こう言いました。

はい yes
将軍様 General [*sama* is polite]
お願いいたします please (polite); it is my wish (that you do that)
青くなっている becoming blue (in the face)
と *to*—and doing that... [here it acts as a conjunction that ties the two phrases together]
こう言いました said thusly

「絵に描いた虎を将軍様が追い出せないなら、私も虎を捕まえることはできません。」

絵に描いた虎 the tiger painted in the picture
将軍様 General [*sama* is polite]
追い出せないなら if (you) can't drive out (the tiger)
私も I also; me too
虎 tiger
を direct object marker
捕まえること the act of capturing [the koto makes a verb into a noun]
できません cannot; not able to

「うーん、まいった。」将軍様は、一休さんの賢さにたいへん感心したということです。

おしまい。

うーん umm...; uh
まいった I'm beat
一休さん Ikkyu
賢さ level of wisdom; cleverness [the *ni* adds the idea of "regarding (the Ikkyu's cleverness)"]
たいへん very
感心した impressed
ということです and that's that
おしまい the end

Ikkyu-san Grammatical Notes

むかし、むかし、一休さんというとても賢いお坊さんがいました。
A long time ago, there lived a very bright young priest called Ikkyu.

むかし、むかし *mukashi, mukashi*
Once upon a time [a common way to start a fairy tale that literally means, "long time ago, long time ago]

という *to iu*
This often introduces someone or something and then a fuller description of that someone or something follows.

いました *imashita*
lived; there was [*imashita* is used with living things and *arimashita* is for inanimate objects.]

小さいころから、賢くてりこうだと評判でした。
From the time he was small, he was famous for his wisdom.

小さいころから *chīsai koro kara*
From childhood [literally, from about the time (he was) small. Another way to say this is *kodomo no koro kara*—from the time (he was) a child. (this appears a line or two below this one in the story) ころ *koro* sets the time frame but also means "about" or "approximately" so you shouldn't use it for exact dates or very recent events.]

評判 *hyōban*

fame; reputation [notice the qualities that describe what he is famous for comes before *hyōban*.]

一休さんの賢さの評判を聞いた将軍様は

The general who had heard of the fame of the wisdom of Ikkyu...

評判を聞いた将軍 *hyōban wo kiita shōgun*

The general who had heard the fame. [I translated the above phrase awkwardly, but it may help your understanding of the sentence structure. In English, I started with "the general" because that is the topic of the sentence (the word behind は *wa*). Work your way backwards in Japanese to see how the information unfolds: shogun -> 聞いた heard (heard what?) 評判 fame (what kind of fame?) 賢さ wisdom (whose wisdom?) 一休さん Ikkyu.]

困らせてやろうと思って

(The general) thought to test (Ikkyu)

困らせてやろう *komarasete yarō*

To put (someone) on the spot [This is the ~*te* form of 困らせる which means to trouble, test, or embarrass someone. *yarō* means to do or put into action.]

ある日、一休さんを お城に呼んで、こう言いました。

One day, he called Ikkyu to the castle and said...

ある日 *aru hi*

One day [adding ある before certain nouns elements adds "some" or "one": ある時 one time; ある場所 some place; ある人 somebody]

お城に呼んで *oshiro ni yonde*

Called to the castle [The に shows the direction Ikkyu

was called to.]

こう言いました kō īmashita
Said in this way [こう means "in this way" or "thus": こう歩いて walk this way; こうやって do like this]

そちに頼みたいことがあるのだが。
To you, I have a favor to ask.

そちに sochi ni
To you [Literally, "to there (where you are standing)"]

頼みたいこと tanomitai koto
a favor [頼む is a verb that means to ask something of someone; 〜たい adds the meaning of "want to"; こと makes the verb into a noun: a thing (I) want to ask = a favor]

そういって、一枚のびょうぶを見せました。
Saying that, (he) showed (Ikkyu) one folding screen.

一枚のびょうぶ ichi mai no byōbu
one folding screen [A byobu is a thin, flat object and therefore like paper or a photograph, use 枚 mai to count it.

見せました misemashita
was shown [見ました saw; 見せました was shown]

一匹の虎が描かれていました。
There was one tiger drawn.

一匹の虎 ippiki no tora
one tiger [Most animals take the counter 匹 (*hiki*, *piki*, *biki* depending on the number)]

描かれていました kakarete imashita
was drawn [The passive form of 描く *kaku*—to draw,

paint, or sketch]

毎晩抜け出して
Every night (the tiger) sneaks out.

毎晩 *mai ban*

Every night [Other examples using 毎 *mai* (every ~): 毎日 *mai nichi*—every day; 毎年 *mai toshi*—every year; 毎月曜日 *mai getsuyōbi*—every Monday;]

抜け出して *nuke dashite*

slip out; sneak away; to break out [This compound word combines 抜く (to extract; to draw out) with 出す (to take out; get out; to show).]

いたずらをするので、困っている
(the tiger) does mischief, therefore (I am) troubled.

いたずら *itazura*

mischief; prank; practical joke [This is most often used in relation to children's pranks or bad behavior, but other uses by adults include practical jokes or defamation.]

ので *node*

that being the case; because of that; therefore [Use ので when giving a reason for an effect. Because of A, B.]

しばらく考えてからこう言いました。
After some thought, (he) said this.

しばらく考えてから *shibaraku kangaete kara*

After thinking a while [Literally, short while > thinking about > from (that time); again, it is often helpful to start at the end of a phrase and work your way back. From the time (he) thought a little.]

立ち上がって頭にねじりはちまきをしめ
Standing up and tying his headband around his head...

立ち上がって *tachi agatte*
Standing up [This is combining 立つ (to stand; to rise) with 上がる (to rise; to go up); combining two similar words emphasizes the action]

頭にねじりはちまき *atama ni nejiri hachimaki*
The headband twisted around (his) head [Again, starting from the end helps understanding. We are talking about the headband (はちまき) that is twisted (ねじり) around the head (頭に).]

将軍様は、びっくりして、「なんじゃと、絵に描いた虎を追い出せというのか？」
The shogun said with surprise, "What? You want me to drive the painted tiger out?"

びっくりして *bikkuri shite*
Surprised (he said...) [The word びっくり (surprise) is enough to introduce the quote.]

なんじゃと *nanja to*
What?! [The emphatic なんじゃ followed by the particle used for quotes と]

というのか？ *to iu no ka?*
Is that what you mean?

将軍様が青くなっていると、一休さんは、こう言いました。
Upon (seeing) the Shogun's face turn blue, Ikkyu said...

青くなっていると *aoku natte iru to*
upon turning blue [The と means "if" or "when" such and such happens]

こう言いました *kō īmashita*
said this [The こう means "in this way" or "thus."]

将軍様が追い出せないなら
If the Shogun cannot drive out...

追い出せない *oi dasenai*
cannot drive out [This combines 追う (to chase; to run after) with 出す (to take out; to put out); the potential form (出せる) expresses the ability to do something. In this case, "CANnot drive out."]

Ikkyū-san in Japanese

一休(いっきゅう)さん

むかし、むかし、一休(いっきゅう)さんというとても賢(かしこ)いお坊(ぼう)さんがいました。小(ちい)さいころから、賢(かしこ)くてりこうだと評判(ひょうばん)でした。これは、一休(いっきゅう)さんが子供(こども)のころのお話(はなし)です。

一休(いっきゅう)さんの賢(かしこ)さの評判(ひょうばん)を聞(き)いた将軍様(しょうぐんさま)は、一休(いっきゅう)さんを困(こま)らせてやろうと思(おも)って、ある日一休(ひいっきゅう)さんをお城(しろ)に呼(よ)んで、こう言(い)いました。

「一休さん、そちに頼みたいことがあるのだが。」そういって、一枚の屏風を見せました。その屏風には、一匹の虎が描かれていました。

「この虎が、毎晩抜け出していたずらをするので、困っている。なんとか、この虎を捕まえたいのだ。」

絵に描いた虎を捕まえることなんて、できるわけがありません。一休さんは、しばらく考えてからこう言いました。

「かしこまりました。」一休さんは、立ち上がって頭にねじりはちまきをしめ、なわをもって屏風の前に立ちました。

「将軍様、私は用意ができました。いつでも虎を捕まえましょう。さあ、将軍様、その屏風の虎をそこから追い出してください。」

将軍様は、びっくりして、「なんじゃと、絵に描いた虎を追い出せというのか？」

「はい、将軍様。お願いいたします。」

将軍様が青くなっていると、一休さんは、こう言いました。

「絵に描いた虎を将軍様が追い出せないなら、私も虎を捕まえることはできません。」

「うーん、まいった。」将軍様は、一休さんの賢さにたいへん感心したということです。

おしまい。

Ikkyū-san in English

一休さん

A long time ago, there was a very bright young monk named Ikkyu. From his youth, he was well known for his wisdom. This is a story from Ikkyu's childhood.

The Shogun heard of Ikkyu's wisdom and thought to test him. One day, he called Ikkyu to the castle and said, "Ikkyu, I have a favor to ask." Saying that, he showed Ikkyu one folding screen (*byobu*). That folding screen had one tiger painted on it.

"This tiger escapes every night and because of that, we are troubled. I want you to catch the tiger."

Of course, there was no possible way to catch a painted in the picture tiger. Ikkyu thought for a while and said, "Yes, sir."

Ikkyu stood up, tightened his headband, and holding a rope, stood in front of the folding screen.

"Shogun, I am ready. Let's catch the tiger any time. Well then, Shogun, drive out that tiger from the folding screen."

The Shogun was surprised and said, "What? You want me to drive a painted tiger out of the picture?"

"Yes, Shogun. Please."

Seeing the Shogun's face turn blue, Ikkyu said, "If

the Shogun is not able to drive out the painted tiger from the picture, I also am not able to catch the tiger."

"Ah, you got me."

The Shogun was quite impressed by Ikkyu's wisdom.

The end.

VOCABULARY

「」 quotation marks

A
開ける　*akeru*　to open
穴　*ana*　hole
青くなっている　*aoku natteiru*　becoming blue (in the face)
ある日　*aru hi*　one day
あるところに　*aru tokoro ni*　some place
頭　*atama*　head
頭にねじりはちまきをしめ　*atama ni nejiri hachimaki wo shime*　tightening the headband around his head

B
美人　*bijin* beautiful woman
びっくり　*bikkuri*　surprised
びっくりして　*bikkuri shite*　being surprised...
びっくりして言いました　*bikkuri shite īmashita*　surprised, he said…
びくともしない　*biku to mo shinai*　does not budge an inch; unmovable
びょうぶ　*byōbu*　a folding screen; byobu

C
小さいころ　*chīsai koro*　when one was a child; childhood
チュー吉　*chu-kichi*　Chukichi [boy mouse name]

D
だが　*da ga*　but [a polite way to soften a request.]
誰　*dare* who

誰でしょう　*dare deshō*　who could it be?
だろう　*darō* I suppose
出かけていきました　*dekakete ikimashita*　left; went
できません　*dekimasen*　cannot; not able to
できる　*dekiru*　being able to do
でも　*demo*　but
でてくれば　*detekureba*　if comes out
どうか　*dōka* please [a little more pleading than どうぞ]
どこか　*dokoka*　somewhere
どうぞ　*dōzo*　please

E

へ　*e*　to
へ行きました　*e ikimashita*　went to …
絵に　*e ni*　in the picture
絵に描いた虎　*e ni kaita tora*　the tiger painted in the picture
へ　*e*　to; the direction of
偉い　*erai*　important

F

夫婦　*fūfu*　husband and wife
吹けば　*fukeba*　if blows [風が吹く *kaze ga fuku* wind blows]
吹き飛ばされてしまう　*fuki tobasarete shimau*　blow completely away
二人　*futari*　the couple

G

が　*ga*　[particle that often marks the subject]
がある　*ga aru*　(I) have (a request)
〜がいました　*ga imashita*　there lived; there was…

H

はちまき	hachi maki	headband
はい	hai	yes
一人	hitori	one person
一人娘	hitori musume	one and only daughter
ほしい	hoshī	want; desire
評判	hyōban	fame; reputation

I

一枚	ichi mai	one (byobu)
一番	ichiban	#1; the best; -est
一番偉い人	ichiban erai hito	greatest person (in the world)
一休さん	ikkyū san	Ikkyu
いくら吹いても	ikura fuitemo	however much (I) blow
言いました	īmashita	said
一匹	ippiki	one (tiger) [hiki/biki/piki is the counter for animals]
いたずら	itazura	prank; mischief; tricking
いつでも	itsu demo	whenever
いつも	itsumo	always
いつも自慢ばかり	itsumo jiman bakari	always bragging (about daughter)

J
自慢　*jiman*　pride; boast(ing)

K
壁　*kabe* wall
壁さん　*kabe san* wall [Mr. Wall]
壁さんのところ　*kabesan no tokoro* where the wall is
描いた　*kaita*　drawn
描いた虎　*kaita tora* the painted tiger
描かれていました　*kakarete imashita* was drawn
隠れてしまう　*kakurete shimau* completely hidden
かなわない　*kanawanai*　cannot match; be no match for
考えて　*kangaete* thinking [考える *kangaeru* to think]
感心した　*kanshin shita* impressed
顔　*kao* face
から　*kara* because [after explanation]
賢い　*kashikoi*　wise
賢くてりこう　*kashikokute rikō*　wise and clever [*kashikoi* is paired with the similar-in-meaning 利口 *rikō* wise; clever; intelligent]
かしこまりました　*kashikomarimashita*　understood; roger
賢さ　*kashikosa* level of wisdom [〜さ indicates a degree or condition of something]
賢さの評判　*kashikosa no hyōban*　reputation for having wisdom
かわいがっていました　*kawaigatteimashita*　loved; tender loving care [from かわいがる *kawaigaru*]
風　*kaze* wind
風さん　*kaze san*　Mr. Wind
結婚　*kekkon*　marriage
結婚させよう　*kekkon saseyō* let's marry her off
きだてのいい　*kidate no ī*　good natured; kindhearted

聞いた　*kīta*　heard [past tense of 聞く *kiku* to listen]
子　*ko*　child
こう　*kō*　like this
こう言いました　*kō īmashita*　said the following
子供のころ　*kodomo no koro*　childhood
困らせてやろう　*komarasete yarō*　to try to trouble (Ikkyu) [*komarasete* to trouble with questions; to test + *yarō* to do; to give (trouble)]
困っている　*komatte iru*　was troubled
この　*kono* this
これは　*kore wa*　as for this (story)
ことになりました　*koto ni narimashita* the matter (marriage) happened
ことにしました　*koto ni shimashita*　was decided
雲　*kumo*　cloud
雲のところ　*kumo no tokoro*　the Cloud's place; Where the cloud is
雲さん　*kumo san* clouds [Mr. Cloud]
雲さんにはかなわない　*kumosan niwa kanawanai*　I'm no match for the clouds.
雲さんのところ　*kumosan no tokoro* the Cloud's place; Where the cloud is

M

前に　*mae ni*　in front of
毎晩　*maiban*　every night
まいった　*maitta*　I'm beat
見合わせて　*mi awasete*　look at each other
見せました　*misemashita*　showed
もちろん　*mochiron* of course
もちろんですとも　*mochiron desu tomo*　of course! To be sure!
もって　*motte*　holding (the rope)
むかし、むかし　*mukashi mukashi*　a long time ago
娘　*musume* daughter

娘のチュー子　*musume no chu-ko* a daughter named Chu-ko
娘をお嫁にもらってください　*musume wo oyome ni moratte kudasai*　please take (our) daughter as a bride

N

なーんだ　*na-n da*　What?!
なんじゃと　*nanjato*　what's that? [*nanja* is colloquial for *nan desu ka* (what's that?) and the *to* is a particle used for quoting and here, to indicate a question.]
なんて　*nante*　(exclamation; emphatic) how …!
なんとか　*nantoka*　somehow; one way or another
なわ　*nawa*　rope; cord
ね　*ne*　[sentence ender used for emphasis]
ねじり　*nejiri*　twist
ねずみ　*nezumi*　mouse
ねずみのチュー子さん　*nezumi no chu-ko san*　the mouse Chuko
ねずみのお父さん　*nezumi no otōsan*　the father mouse
になった　*ni natta*　became [〜になる ~ni naru to become]
にはかなわない　*niwa kanawanai*　no match against…
のだ　*no da*　(explanatory ender + copula)
のか　*no ka*　[ender showing a realization of the truth)]
ので　*node*　therefore
抜け出して　*nuke dashite*　sneak out; slip away

O

お父さん　*o tōsan*　father
お坊さん　*obōsan*　priest; monk; young boy
お話　*ohanashi*　story (polite)
追い出せ　*oi dase*　drive out (imperative)
追い出せないなら　*oi dasenai nara*　if (you) can't drive out (the tiger)
追い出してください　*oi dashite kudasai*　please chase (it) out

お母さん　*okāsan*　mother
お願いいたします　*onegai itashimasu*　please (polite); it is my wish (that you do that)
おしまい　*oshimai*　the end
お城に　*oshiro ni*　castle (honorific)
お嫁　*oyome*　bride
お嫁にもらってください　*oyome ni moratte kudasai*　please take (daughter) as a bride
お嫁にやる　*oyome ni yaru*　give one's daughter in marriage

S

さあ　*saa*　well, then; all right...
賛成　*san sei*　agreement; approval
賛成して言いました　*sansei shite īmashita*　agreeing, she said...
世界で　*sekai de*　in the world
世界で一番偉い人　*sekai de ichiban erai hito*　the world's greatest man
世界で一番えらい太陽さん　*sekai de ichiban erai taiyō san*　Oh Sun, who is the greatest in the world...
しばらく　*shibaraku*　a while; some time
しばらく考えてから　*shibaraku kangaete kara*　after thinking a while
しめ　*shime*　tighten; bind
将軍様　*shōgun sama*　general (honorific)
そういって　*sō itte*　saying that...
そちに　*sochi ni*　for you [*sochi* means there or that way, but in this case, the shogun is referring to Ikkyu.]
相談　*sōdan*　consult; talk it over
そこで　*soko de*　then
そこから　*soko kara*　from there
そこで　*sokode*　then
その　*sono*　that (byobu)
そのびょうぶの虎　*sono byōbu no tora*　the tiger in that

folding screen
それは　　sore wa　　as for that
そして　　soshite　　and then
すっかり　　sukkari　　completely
少し　　sukoshi　　a little
少し考えてから　　sukoshi kangaete kara　　after thinking a little...
住んでいました　　sunde imashita　　there lived...

T

立ち上がって　　tachi agatte　　standing... [this is combining *tachi* (stand) with *agaru* (raising) in the ~te form]
立ちました　　tachimashita　　stood
たいへん　　taihen　　very
太陽　　taiyō　　the sun
太陽に会うと　　taiyō ni au to　　upon meeting the sun...
太陽のところ　　taiyō no tokoro　　the sun's place; where the sun is
太陽さん　　taiyō san　　the sun [Mr. Sun]
頼みたいこと　　tanomitai koto　　a request
と　　to　　and
という　　to iu　　"such a"; (describing ikkyuu-san)
ということです　　to iu koto desu　　and that's that
というのか　　to iu no ka　　are you saying...? [*to iu* saying or such a thing and the emphatic ender *noka*.]
と結婚してほしい　　to kekkon shite hoshī　　want (daughter) to get married to (greatest man)
と結婚する　　to kekkon suru　　get married to...
と思って　　to omotte　　(he) thought
〜とも　　tomo　　certainly; of course
隣村　　tonari mura　　the next village
とんでもない　　tondemonai　　absurd; preposterous
虎　　tora　　tiger
年頃　　toshigoro　　of (marriageable) age
とても　　totemo　　very

とても美人　totemo bijin　a very beautiful woman
捕まえましょう　tsukamaemashō　let's capture (the tiger)
捕まえること　tsukamaeru koto　(the act of) capturing
捕まえたい　tsukamaetai　want to capture
って　tte　[casual topic marker]

U

うーん　u-n—yes?; hmm

W

わ　wa　[sentence ender used by women]
わけがありません　wake ga arimasen　have to reason (to be able to)
私　watashi　I
私も　watashi mo　I also; me too
私に　watashi ni　in me
私に穴を開けてしまう　watashi ni ana wo akete shimau　(mouse) opens holes in me
私は　watashi wa　as for me…
私はねずみさんにはかなわない　watashi wa nezumi san ni wa kanawanai　I'm no match for the Mouse
を　wo　[direct object marker]

Y

やはり　yahari　not surprisingly; as expected
用意　yōi　preparations
用意ができました　yōi ga dekimashita　I'm ready; I'm prepared
嫁　yome　bride
呼んで　yonde　called (to the castle)

DOWNLOAD LINK

Please go to this website to download the MP3s for these stories:

http://japanesereaders.com/1028

(You can also sign up for our newsletter to get more free stuff!)

Thank you for purchasing and reading this book! To contact the authors, please email them at help@thejapanshop.com. See also the wide selection of materials for learning Japanese at www.TheJapanShop.com and the free site for learning Japanese www.thejapanesepage.com.

Thank you for your purchase!

Did you know most of our digital eBooks are available in money-saving bundles?

Check them out at https://www.thejapanshop.com/bundles

Printed in Great Britain
by Amazon

19965286R00047